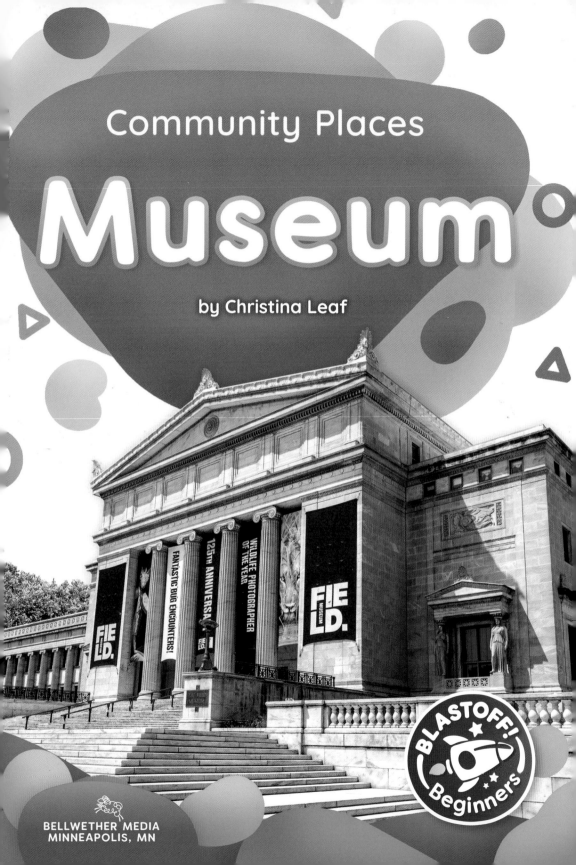

Community Places

Museum

by Christina Leaf

BELLWETHER MEDIA
MINNEAPOLIS, MN

BLASTOFF!
Beginners

Blastoff! Beginners are developed by literacy experts and educators to meet the needs of early readers. These engaging informational texts support young children as they begin reading about their world. Through simple language and high frequency words paired with crisp, colorful photos, Blastoff! Beginners launch young readers into the universe of independent reading.

Blastoff! Universe

Reading Level — Grade K

Grades 1-3

Grade 4

Sight Words in This Book 🔍

a	has	look	these
about	have	many	they
are	how	one	this
at	in	some	to
for	is	the	we
go	it	there	which

This edition first published in 2023 by Bellwether Media, Inc.

No part of this publication may be reproduced in whole or in part without written permission of the publisher. For information regarding permission, write to Bellwether Media, Inc., Attention: Permissions Department, 6012 Blue Circle Drive, Minnetonka, MN 55343.

Library of Congress Cataloging-in-Publication Data

LC record for Museum available at: https://lccn.loc.gov/2022036353

Text copyright © 2023 by Bellwether Media, Inc. BLASTOFF! BEGINNERS and associated logos are trademarks and/or registered trademarks of Bellwether Media, Inc.

Editor: Rebecca Sabelko   Designer: Gabriel Hilger

Printed in the United States of America, North Mankato, MN.

Table of Contents

At the Museum!

Look at
this painting!
We are at
the museum!

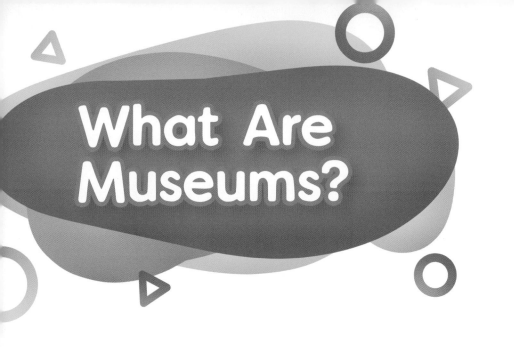

What Are Museums?

Museums are places to learn! There are many kinds.

Many have
special things.
They keep
these things safe.

Some have **guides**.
They give **tours**.

guide

tour

11

Many Kinds

Which kind
should we go to?
This one has art.

This one is
for **science**.
It shows how
things work.

This one is
in a house!
It teaches
about **history**.

This one is
about the earth.
It has dinosaurs!

dinosaur

This one is for kids!
We love to learn
at museums!

Museum Facts

At the Museum

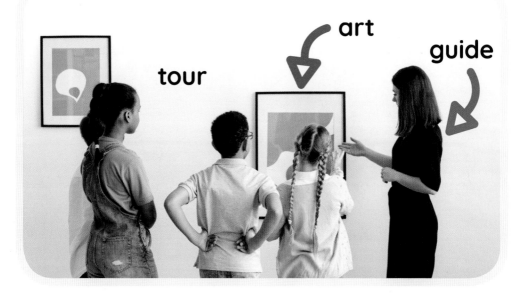

tour

art

guide

What Happens at a Museum?

look at art

learn how things work

learn about history

Glossary

guides

people who give
tours at museums

history

the study of
the past

science

the study
of how the
world works

tours

times when a
person shows
others around

To Learn More

ON THE WEB

FACTSURFER

Factsurfer.com gives you a safe, fun way to find more information.

1. Go to www.factsurfer.com.

2. Enter "museum" into the search box and click 🔍.

3. Select your book cover to see a list of related content.

Index

The images in this book are reproduced through the courtesy of: S-F, front cover; Krakenimages.com, p. 3; Sergio Azenha/ Alamy, pp. 4-5; Puwadol Jaturawutthichai, p. 6; Ekpluto, pp. 6-7; monkeybusinessimages, pp. 8-9; Popova Valeriya, pp. 10-11, 23 (guides, tours); Kiev.Victor, pp. 12-13; cowardlion, pp. 14-15; :KenWiedemann, pp. 16-17; elRoce, pp. 18-19; Jeffrey Isaac Greenberg 3+/ Alamy, pp. 20-21; SeventyFour, p. 22 (at the museum); South_agency, p. 22 (look at art); frantic00, p. 22 (learn how things work); 1000 Photography, p. 22 (learn about history); legacy1995, p. 23 (history); Monkey Business Images, p. 23 (science).